GOD
and
THE LAW
of
ATTRACTION

DeCarlo A. Eskridge

NU DAE Enterprise Publications

United States of America

*Amazon — **Create**Space*
ISBN-13: 978-1463644734
ISBN-10: 1463644736

Edited by Objective Eye Editing Services
Cover Design ©NU DAE Enterprises, LLC, 2011
DeCarloEskridge.com

Printed in the United States of America

CONTENTS

Acknowledgement

This book is dedicated with love to my best friend and lovely wife, Amanda. Without your tireless collaboration, encouragement and understanding this book would not be possible. I would be remiss not to mention Missi, our wonderful Yorkshire Terrier, who fills our lives with so much joy.

I would also like to thank you, my reader. Your desire to read such a book it has brought about its manifestation. It has been deliberately condensed to make it as easy as possible to read, comprehend, and use. It is my solemn belief that all who read this book and practice the principles herein will begin to undergo a metamorphosis of radical proportion, and experience life beyond their wildest dreams.

THE AUTHOR

"If one advances confidently in the direction of his dreams, and endeavors to live the life which he has imagined, he will meet with success unexpected in common hours."

~Henry David Thoreau

Introduction

The book you are about to read is called *God and the Law of Attraction*. Its goal is to awaken the divine giant within you. For the next few hours, I will be your spiritual life coach on this spiritual journey. I will be using a seven-step process called the *CREATOR*. We will discuss the *CREATOR* process in greater detail further along in the book. Let's get started!

What price would you pay for success? We all desire to be successful and to excel in the various areas of our lives: personal, family, financial, social, spiritual, emotional, physical, as well as professional. But without the proper tools, success is short-lived and, most often, illusive.

What is "success?" Some say, "Success is the progressive realization of a noteworthy goal." But what does success mean to you? A wise man once said that the best way to predict the future is present thinking. Change your thinking and change your world.

Repeat the following affirmations
throughout the day for the next 21 days.

I Don't Just C.O.P.E.

I Am __COMMITTED__ to my SUCCESS.

I Am __OPEN__ to my SUCCESS.

I __PARTICIPATE__ in my SUCCESS.

I Am __EXCITED__ about my SUCCESS.

Idle Thoughts

"There is no more self-contradictory concept than that of 'idle thoughts.' What gives rise to the perception of a whole world can hardly be called idle."

~A Course in Miracles

"As a man thinks in his heart, so is he."
Proverbs 23:7

Jesus said that on the Day of Judgment we will give an account for every idle word. We misunderstand the Day of Judgment to be some dreaded future day. But many of us are at this very moment reaping the harvest of our past thoughts, words and actions. The Day of Judgment is already upon us.

And if we desire something different, if we desire a life of abundance, we need to begin this moment to be accountable for our state, thoughts, words and actions.

"Blame is an escape from responsibility and a way to give away your power. When you can see and take responsibility for your part in events, things will change. Responsibility is not a weight to carry, but a key to reclaiming your power."

~Dr. Michael Ryce

Allow me to share with you the "Responsibility Creed"

RESPONSIBILITY CREED

I am responsible for how I see.

What I seek is what I receive.

I choose those feelings I experience.

Within myself I find deliverance.

I decide those goals I will achieve.

What I will be is up to me.

All that I am, I've asked for.

I need only to ask if I desire more.

I am responsible; I now understand.

As I think, so I am.

"Our response is a conscious choice. When we re-act, we are unconsciously driven by our past. Respond-ability is the ability to respond rather than re-act."
~Dr. Michael Ryce

The 7 Steps of Personal Creation

We are now going to cover a seven-step personal creation process. In this seven-step process, we will spell out the acronym "CREATOR."

The letter "**C**" stands for "Consciousness."

The letter "**R**" stands for "Release."

The letter "**E**" stands for "Expansion."

The letter "**A**" stands for "Allowing."

The letter "**T**" stands for "Transformation."

The letter "**O**" stands for "Opulence."

The letter "**R**" stands for "Re-creation."

"If you advance confidently in the direction of your dreams, and endeavor to live the life you have imagined, you will meet with the success unexpected in common hours."

~Henry David Thoreau

You are now ready to embark on a journey that will radically transform your life forever—if you let it. Remember: as with any book, seminar, workshop, motivational speaker, preacher or teacher—it doesn't matter; all motivation or motive of action begins within. No one can make you change; only you can begin the process of change in your life. But we will, in fact, give you the tools needed for personal transformation.

I am excited about the journey we're about to embark upon!

What is Creativity?

Creativity is one's ability to generate new ideas or to conceive of new perspectives on existing ideas–in short, the ability to create something from one's own imagination.

God said, "Let Us make man in our image, after our likeness: and let them have dominion over…all the earth."

So why do so many of us fail to experience lives of purposeful existence?

The Moment of Discovery

Through "God and the Law of Attraction," you will discover the tools needed for success and consciously live the life for which you were destined. Again, the choice is yours. Do not allow another moment to go by without making a decision to change.

This is where I come in—your spiritual coach. I utilize a tool called **M**ental **I**magery **N**euro **D**ynamics, also known as M.I.N.D. Mechanics, to assist you in reaching your life-long goals and discovering your divine potential. M.I.N.D. Mechanics utilizes the tools of self-visualization, actualization, and realization to assist you in creating the life you have always desired.

The Word of God has a great deal to say about right thinking. One Scripture says, "As a man thinks in his heart, so is he" (Proverbs 3:27). My goal as your spiritual life coach is to assist you on the track of right thinking, so that you might experience the life that you were destined to live.

As your spiritual life coach, I will assist you in living the life that God has destined for you. Many of us fail to live that life because we do not believe that it is available to us, and that is about to change.

We are now ready to step into the first portion of the creation process of "God and the Law of Attraction." This portion of the process called "Consciousness."

CONSCIOUSNESS

Understanding Your Identity as a Creator

- Identify Creator-like characteristics

- Outline the personality of the Creator

- Discuss your Creator-like attributes

- Define the benefits of being a Creator

The Characteristics of the Creator

The source of all creation is pure **LOVE** consciousness seeking expression from the spiritual to the physical realm. When we realize that our true Self is one of unlimited **LOVE** potentiality and possibility, we align ourselves with the Creator God (**LOVE**) and begin a life of limitless possibilities. And we, like Jesus, will say, "I and the Father are one" (John 10:30).

The Personality of the Creator

The personality of God is love, joy, peace, longsuffering, gentleness, goodness, faithfulness, grace, mercy and compassion, to name a few. God has placed within the souls of men hearts capable of feelings and emotions such as love and compassion. God wants us to love what He loves and hate what He hates. God wants us to love Him with all our hearts, our souls and our minds, and to love our neighbors as ourselves. This is the personality of the Creator.

Your Creator-like Attributes
(Divine Nature Attributes)

We, like God, are spiritual beings clothed in humanity—what I call "earth suits." We are most like God when we are creating out of a spirit of LOVE. Jesus said that you will know them by their fruit. Put on the fruits of the Spirit, such as love, joy, peace, longsuffering, gentleness, goodness, faith, meekness and temperance. And the Bible says, "against such there is no law" (Galatians 5:22-23).

Now what does that mean, that there is no law? We are operating out of the fruit of the Spirit. We're fulfilling the law. Christ said that the law and the prophets rest upon two commandments—to love the Lord your God with all your heart, your soul and your mind, and to love your neighbor as yourself.

Most of us really don't consider how powerful these commandments are: "Love the Lord thy God with all thy soul, thy heart and thy mind," and "Love thy neighbor as thyself." What we fail to understand is that we say, "Well, I love God, but

I can't stand that person over there." The truth of the matter is, we can't hate another and love God. We can't hate another and love ourselves. To the extent that we love others, it shows how much we love ourselves. It shows how much we love God. We fail to recognize that we are all connected. And if I hate my brother, I hate myself, because I am a part of the same divine body, and that's the body of God.

Now don't misunderstand me. I am not talking about religion. Everything in the universe is God's. Now, why is this? It is because in Him we live and have our being. It is because of God that the trees exist. It is because of God that I exist. And if God ceases to exist, so will I. Without the Divine Dreamer, there can be no dream.

Many of us go to sleep at night and dream. Some of us have nightmares. But the moment we wake up, everything that existed in that dream no longer exists.

Now, let us expand on this concept for a moment. If God were to cease from existing, everything linked with God would cease to exist. And we are a part of that "everything." We're like cells in the divine body of God. And when we are operating and living as we should, in righteousness and right living, then we prosper. But when we live contrary, we become cancerous cells in the body of God. And it's only as we align ourselves for the purpose of God that there is order in our lives.

Many of us live a lifestyle short of God's best (sin), primarily because we are out of order with the divine decree of love that God has set forth. Who would know better how we are to live but the Creator of the mind, body, spirit and the universe? What is sin? Sin is anything not of faith or living a lifestyle anything short of love. God is love, and when you walk in the mind of Christ, you fulfill the law of love. You are an expression of Divine presence; the Christ within and creation is your birthright.

We are a part of the divine Creator of the universe, so my challenge to you is this: if you are not happy in your personal life, in your family life, in your financial life, in your social life, in your spiritual life, in your emotional life, in your physical life, or in your professional life, then I challenge you, creator, to create something new. Only you can create your perfect world. Not God, nor man; only *you* can create your perfect world.

Benefits of Being a Creator

Now I will give you the keys of creation. Jesus said, "I will give you the keys of the kingdom of heaven. Whatever you bind or declare impossible on the earth [or what we call the physical realm] will be bound or declared impossible in the heavens [or in the mental/spiritual realm]; and whatever you loose or declare possible on the earth [or in the physical realm] will be loosed or declared possible in the heavens [or the mental/spiritual realm]."

What does that mean? Do we determine what happens in heaven? Far be it! But what happens is heaven agrees with us. And what I mean by that is if I say continuously throughout my day, "This is going to be a bad day," Heaven says "Be it unto you according to your faith." If I say to myself continuously, "I'll never amount to anything," Heaven says, "be it unto you according to your faith."

Now, Heaven's desire for me is something far greater than I can see for myself. Heaven says that it has for me more than I can ask, think or imagine. Heaven says mine eye has not seen, nor has it entered into the imagination of men the things that God has for them. But if I, like those raised up in the community of Jesus, don't believe, then Jesus through his Spirit will not be able to perform many miracles in my life because of my unbelief. We have a church today that says, "The miracles have gone out with the apostles." And Heaven says, "Be it unto you according to your faith." We have a church today that says, "Poverty is next to godliness," and Heaven says, "Be it unto you according to your faith." We have a church today that says, "God afflicts us with illness, lack, loss and limitations." And Heaven says, "Be it unto you according to your faith."

Are you beginning to understand the power of your words? We have said some things in the body of Christ, according to the tradition of men, which do not line up with the Word of God. We must begin to speak what the Word says and not what man says. Jesus dealt with this same dilemma in his day, so much so that the religious leaders, who wanted to maintain their religious reputation, crucified the Lord of Glory.

Are we, because of religion, crucifying the Lord of Glory? Is it because of our beliefs that we fail to live the more abundant life? Is it because of our beliefs that we fail to live a life of wisdom, wellness and wealth? Are we, because of our beliefs, failing to touch and change and transform the world around us? Have we become the modern day Pharisees?

Let us not seek religion, but a relationship with the Creator of the universe. Let our relationship be founded upon the two commandments—to love the Lord thy God with all thy heart, thy soul and thy mind, and loving thy neighbor as ourselves.

RECAP
CONSCIOUSNESS

- We identified Creator-like characteristics

- We outlined the personality of the Creator

- We discussed your Creator-like attributes

- We defined the benefits of being a Creator

Notes

RELEASE

Discover How
Destructive Erroneous Views In Limitation
Shape Your Destiny

- Define Release and the 5 types of Release

- Identify the 3 major strongholds every-one encounters

- Overcome strongholds using positive affirmations

DEFINE RELEASE

We are now ready to discuss the "Release" process. We will discuss how we allow destructive, erroneous views of our life shape our destiny. In this section, we will define "Release" and the five types of Release, as well as the three major strongholds that we all encounter sometimes in our lives. Finally, we will discuss how to overcome these strongholds using positive affirmations.

The essence of true Release is exchanging our vision of reality for God's vision of reality. In Releasing, we are free from our past (or memory) as well as the present (or the familiar), which is nothing more than the prison of past conditioning. And in our willingness to step into the future (imagination—the field of all possibilities), we surrender ourselves to the creative mind of God who has orchestrated on our behalf the boundless potentiality of the universe.

"For the weapons of our warfare are not fleshly, but mighty through God to the pulling down of strongholds; Releasing imaginations, and every high thing that exalts itself against the knowledge of God, and bringing into captivity every thought to the obedience of Christ" (2 Cor 10:4-5).

There are five types of Release that we will discuss in this section. The first Release we simply call **"release"** or **"forgiveness."** Jesus had much to say about forgiveness. He said if you don't forgive your brother his shortcomings, your Heavenly Father will not forgive you of yours.

So the question becomes, "Is God keeping count of how many times you failed to forgive?" Allow me to answer that question for you: certainly not. When God created the universe, He created the universe in such a way that whatever we're sending out returns to us multiplied.

"Forgiveness is about setting you free, not others; in its truest sense, it's the cancellation of your need to be unloving towards others."

Now what does that mean? We'll use the example of a seed. If you plant a seed, do you expect a return of a single seed? Of course not. You expect a harvest from that single seed. Whatever we send out in thought form, through our state, thoughts and emotions, is multiplied in reality. So whatever you send out consciously or unconsciously, its physical equivalent will return to you multiplied. God said that His Word would not return to Him void. Neither will yours, creator. When you truly forgive, you release your need to be unloving towards others.

We must begin to understand that we create, and that we have created the reality that we are presently experiencing. If what I say is true, and I assure you that it is, forgiveness is a must!

The next type of Release that we will discuss is "**repentance**." Another way to think of repentance is changing one's mind. You see, when most people think about repentance, they think of remorse. And they think that if they could just get sad enough, sorrowful enough and pitiful enough that God will forgive them. But God's goal in repentance is a changed mind: to change your mind from your old, erroneous thinking to God's thinking.

You may have said, "How do I know what God is thinking?" We know what God is thinking through His Word. You may recall when Jesus said, "I only do those things that I see the Father doing." How was it that Jesus saw the Father working? He saw the Father working through the Word, and you will see in many cases that Jesus quoted the Word. But if you don't understand the Word of God, then you can't understand what the Father is doing. "Let this mind be in you that is also in Christ Jesus" (Philippians 2:5).

We choose many causes in the world that have nothing to do with the kingdom of God, but are politically correct. We must begin to take up causes that line up with the mind of God, which is "LOVE." Anything that keeps us from walking in love keeps us from the mind of Christ.

So when we talk about repentance, we're talking about changing our minds so that we can begin to think as God thinks; so that we can begin to think like Christ thinks—so that we can unleash the power of the "Christ mind" in our own lives. But we will never do that apart from God's

Word. Paul said it this way: "Let this mind be in you that was also in Christ Jesus." Paul also said, "Renew your mind by the washing of the Word."

We must have the mind of God through the Word of God. It's not enough to pray if we're not abiding by the Word. Some of us are praying for wisdom, but we're not going to the source of all wisdom, and that is the Word of God. If we go to God's Word as little children and we are open to the Spirit, God will begin to reveal His truth to us. And God says that He would not deny anyone who asks for the wisdom of the Spirit. So you need only to ask God for wisdom, and you, like Solomon, will find yourself awakening to the mind of Christ, receiving wellness, wisdom and wealth.

The next type of Release I want to discuss is "**resistance**," or to "**reject**" or cast down. In the book of James, we are told to resist the devil and he will flee from us. But we often fail to consider the most important part of the sentence. It says to resist the devil and he will flee, but draw nigh to God and He will draw nigh unto you.

The key to resistance is to reject the devil (**D**estructive **E**rroneous **V**iews **I**n **L**imitation). And what I don't mean, as so many of us as believers find ourselves doing, having conversations with the devil (negative self-talk), stomping on the devil, or continuously rebuking the devil. We spend more time worshipping the devil (talking) than we do God (**G**ood **O**ne **D**esires). Now you say, "My intention is certainly not to worship the devil." But if the devil is your center of attention, then he gets your worship. Where attention goes, energy flows.

Whatever you focus on expands. If you're focusing on God, if you're praising Him and your meditation is on the goodness, the mercy and the love of God, then you will have little or no time to focus on the devil. We have within us God's creative nature. So remember, whatever you focus on most of the time will be manifested in your life.

God has placed within every human being something called a reticular activating system. This is a complex name for something quite simple. What this means is that we cannot think two opposing thoughts at the same time. And the Word says that a double-minded man is unstable in all his ways. God has designed you in such a way that if you're focusing on God, God is going to expand in your life. If you're focusing on the devil, however, then the devil is going to expand. So whatever you set your attention on will grow.

This brings to mind a story about a Native American fisherman who came to town every Saturday afternoon. He always brought his two dogs with him. One was white and the other was black. He had taught them to fight on command.

Every Saturday afternoon in the town square, the people would gather and these two dogs would fight, and the fisherman would take bets. On one Saturday, the black dog would win; another Saturday, the white dog would win - but the old fisherman always won!

His friends began to ask him how he did it. He said, "Inside each of us resides two dogs. One of the dogs is flesh. The other dog is Spirit. The fleshly dog fights the

*Spiritual dog all of the time." When asked which dog wins, the old man reflected for a moment and replied, "The one you feed the most." ~*Anonymous

So my question to you, creator, is, "What dog are you feeding?" Are you feeding your fleshly dog and is the flesh continuously having victory over your life? Or are you feeding your Spiritual dog, and is your Spirit built up in such a way that when the things of this world begin to challenge you, you're not shaken...you're not moved because you're feeding your Spirit through the words of Truth?

Understand that whatever dog you feed will win the fight. So if you are always feeding the Spiritual dog, he gets bigger and wins the fight, but when you feed the flesh/sin dog, he gets bigger and wins the fight. You determine how successful you're going to be in your life by the dog you feed.

The next type of Release that we want to discuss is that of **"reframing"** or **"refocusing"** one's attention. We have touched on it briefly, and it basically says this: whatever you give your attention to expands. It's important that we begin to set our gaze upon the Creator of the universe, because as we set our gaze upon God, God will begin to expand in our lives in such a way that we will be like Christ. And we will be able to ask the Father whatever it is that we desire, and it will be done unto us because our focus, our gaze and our attention will be set upon Him.

If you set your mind on lack, loss and limitation, then what you will have in your life is lack, loss and limitation. But if you set your mind on wisdom, wellness and wealth, then you will have and find in your life wisdom, wellness and wealth.

My question to you, creator: "What is it that you want to attract in your life?" And then I challenge you to begin to set your gaze upon the thing you desire, not the thing you do not want. As you begin to re-frame and re-focus your attention, you'll begin to see things ushered into your life that you believed at one time impossible to achieve. You'll begin to see prosperity, you'll begin to see relationships renewed, you'll begin to see opportunities, and you will begin to see wealth in everything that you do because your attention will be that of wisdom, wellness and wealth.

The last type of Release is that of "**rest**" or "**relaxation**." Jesus said it this way: "Cast your cares upon me and I will give you rest. Take My yoke upon you and learn of me, and you will find that I am meek and lowly." There is a "rest" that we're to enter into, but it's not a particular holiday; the rest that we enter into as believers is the rest of a personal relationship with the Creator of the universe.

The Pharisees set out to do the law. But in doing the law, they missed out on the fulfillment of the law in the person that stood in their midst. What the law repre-sented (love) was before them in the person of Jesus Christ. As God's children when we fail to walk in love we fall into the error of the Pharisees.

It has been said that God on the seventh day rested from all His works under the Heavens. It has also been said that we are to rest from our labors. But you see, our rest is not meant to be from a given day, but from a person. We're to be like branches on a vine. We have been created to bear much fruit. But apart from Him (Christ), we can do nothing. Paul said it this way, "That I can do all things through Christ who strengthens me, but not I, but Christ in me, the hope of glory."

Resting allows us to live in the fullness of the person of God, through Christ. We begin to realize that we are linked to Christ, the Creator of the universe, and we begin to rest from our works as He works in and through us. You see, resting does not mean that we don't work, that we don't live out God's calling in our lives. But what resting does is allow us to leave the results or the consequences up to God. As we do what it is that God has called us to do, we know that He's going to fulfill His purpose in and through us. So it's no longer "I," but Christ in me, the hope of Glory.

Think of the license plate that you often see that reads, "Christ is my co-pilot." That's not resting. Christ is not working for you, he is working through you. He's not the co-pilot; He's the supreme commander of your soul.

Christ said it this way, "How is it you say that you love Me, but you don't do the things that I say. You call Me Lord, but you go about to carry out your own will." When we are linked to God, we have a pure heart, a perfect heart. A heart that says, "Lord, what is it that you would have me do at this moment?" And we find ourselves in a continual state of obedience to the will of God.

Herein is the secret to the power of the Christ mind. As we take on the spirit of servitude to the Father through the Spirit, we become Christ's ambassadors on the earth. And it is at this moment that we can ask the Father whatever it is that we wish because our mind is linked with His mind. We are of one mind, and it is in this resting that we're empowered to carry out the fullness of the creation process.

We're now ready to discuss the three strongholds: lust of the flesh, pride of life and lust of the eyes. We must overcome all of these before being fully able to walk in the power of the creation process.

"For the weapons of our warfare are not fleshly or carnal or physical, but they are mighty through God for the pulling down of strongholds; releasing imaginations, and every high thing that exalts itself against the knowledge of God, and bringing into captivity every thought to the obedience of Christ" (2 Cor. 10:4-5).

Identify the 3 Major Strongholds

We are not ignorant of the enemy's devices. Therefore, we release those negative areas in our lives through the knowledge gained from Jesus' wilderness experience. We will discuss how to overcome the lust of the flesh, the pride of life and the lust of the eyes.

Releasing Lust of the Flesh

"Turn these stones to bread" (Ex 16:15).

Goal - Physical temptation.

Five Senses – example: Esau and the bowl of soup. (Hebrews 12:16-17)

The primary goal is safety, security and survival.

"Turn these stones to bread," was Satan's first challenge to Jesus in the wilderness. The goal here was a physical temptation. And what you will notice as we graduate through the temptation is how Satan moved from the physical to the mental to the spiritual.

Let's get back to the physical temptation of the five senses. Example: Esau and the bowl of soup. Esau was willing to trade his birthright for a bowl of soup because he was hungry. He despised his own birthright. The primary goal of the physical temptation is that of safety, security and survival. This temptation was focused on the humanity of Jesus, His need for survival. The devil was tempting Jesus at perhaps the weakest point in his life. He tempted Jesus to use His ability to satisfy His hunger after 40 days of fasting. And he asked Him to turn stones to bread.

Jesus certainly had the ability to accomplish this. However, He would have acted based upon His immediate need and would have broken His position of subjection to His Father's will. It was God's will to provide for His needs; not for Him to use His divine power independently.

Often Satan will tempt us after a grand victory or during our weakest moment. As he did with Jesus, he will tempt us to gratify the needs of the flesh. Now certainly, Jesus had the ability to accomplish turning the stones to bread. For He said in the Scriptures, "If you don't praise me, I will make these stones rise up and praise me." However, in this case, Jesus didn't act upon His immediate needs, for He would have broken fellowship with the Father. And Jesus chose God's will over Satan's will. God desires to provide for His children, even as He desired to fulfill Jesus' needs. But it was not the appropriate time. God still had some things that He wanted to reveal to Jesus in that wilderness experience. And feeding his flesh would have taken Him out of the position to receive what God had for Him. So Jesus quoted Scripture when speaking to the devil, and this is how we will also find ourselves victorious. Jesus said, "Man shall not live by bread alone, but by every word that proceeds out of the mouth of God" (Deut 8:3-10).

The next temptation was the pride of life. Satan tempted Jesus by saying, "Cast yourself off the temple and God will give His Angels charge over you, so that you would not even bruise your heel against a stone."

Releasing Pride of Life

"Cast yourself off the temple" (Ps. 91:11-12).

Goal - Self-centeredness (Heart condition).

God's purpose vs. My purpose – example, Moses and the rock (Num 20:10).

The primary goal is "Me-Myself-I."

This goal was mental. It was Jesus' purpose vs. God's purpose. Example: Moses and the children of Israel. You may recall the story. The children of Israel had been complaining, and they said, "Why have you brought us out into this wilderness to kill us? We don't even have any water to drink." So Moses went to the Lord, and the Lord told Moses, "Moses, speak to the rock and I will bring forth water for you and the people of Israel." Moses gathered the congregation and suddenly said, "Must we (being he and Aaron) fetch you water from this rock?" And he struck the rock instead of speaking to the rock. It was because of his disobedience that Moses did not enter into the Promised Land. So Moses had to see the Promised Land from afar.

In this same theme, Satan tempted Jesus to take a shortcut to Glory. He wanted Jesus to cast Himself off the temple, possibly killing Himself, and go to Glory without the persecution and suffering of the cross. But because Jesus fulfilled His purpose, you and I are now empowered to fulfill our purpose because the person of Christ resides within us. By asking Jesus to cast Himself off the pinnacle of the temple, Satan was challenging His dependence on God the Father.

Jesus replied, "You shall not tempt the Lord your God" (Deut 6:16, Ex 17: 1-17 & Num 20:6-13).

Releasing Lust of the Eye

"All of these things I will give you if you worship me" (Ex 20:3-4).

Goal – Spiritual temptation.

Worshiping other gods – example, Nimrod's Tower of Babel (Gen 11:1-9).

The primary goal is to give things preeminence over God.

"All of these things will I give you if you worship me." The temptation is to worship other gods. Example: Nimrod and the Tower of Babel. In Genesis, we find that there is a tower being built. And God said, "Let us go down and see this tower being built." And God said, "These people are of one language and of one mind. If I allow them to continue in their ways, nothing will be impossible for them." However, the goal of the people was not to worship God, but to self-worship. They said, "Let us make a name for ourselves that we would not disappear in the earth or that we would not leave a legacy."

And again, leaving a legacy is an awesome thing. But if your legacy is left and it has no knowledge of God, the Word says: "What does it profit to gain the whole world and to lose your own soul?" So here we find that the primary goal is self-acceptance, worldly acceptance, acceptance of the creation but not the Creator.

The devil took Jesus on the highest mountain and offered Him all the kingdoms of the world in exchange for worship. This was an appeal to worship the creation instead of the Creator, God. It was also an effort to have Jesus submit to the devil's will of immediate rule, or immediate gratification of a world system rule. Satan said this was all his and he would give it to Him.

But the world itself was not, and nor has it ever been, Satan's. God has given all dominion of the world, of the earth, to men. By default, we have given our dominion over to Satan. We can only reclaim dominion as we grow in knowledge. The Word says, "God's people perish for a lack of knowledge."

Growing in the knowledge of who we are is what the creation process is all about...helping you grow in the knowledge to realize that you have power and dominion over the princes of the power of the air and of this world. God has given you dominion through the person of Jesus Christ. And you will be just like those in the New Testament who cast out demons in the name of Jesus.

We have dominion and power in the person of Jesus Christ. And even the devil trembles when we walk in that power. Abundance flows to us. Wisdom is known by us, and wellness is a lifestyle. You are a creator, and only you can create your perfect world, not God, nor man. Only you can create your perfect world.

Jesus replied, "You shall worship the Lord your God and him only will you serve" (Deut 6:13-25 & 8:18-20).

Again, Jesus overcame the devil with a Scripture. He said, "You should worship the Lord your God and Him only should you serve." Jesus reminds us that we overcome **Destructive Erroneous Views In**

Limitation by lovingly subjecting ourselves to the Word of God and rejecting the devil's word. And he must flee from us as we draw near to God, as He draws near to us. And herein is the power of the releasing process.

Overcome the DEVIL Using Positive Affirmations

Here are a few tools to assist you in successfully overcoming **Destructive Erroneous Views In Limitation** using positive affirmations. We utilize a seven-step process called **AFFIRMS**. The "**A**" stands for "**affirm**" in the positive. The "**F**" stands for "**first-person**," I. The next letter, "**F**," means to affirm with "**feelings**," giving your affirmation energy and life. The "**I**" stands for the "**idea**," and must be specific. The "**R**" means to "**remain**" brief. The "**M**" "**must**" be in the present tense. And "**S**" represents "**something better**" of whatever it is that you are affirming; affirm your desire by saying, "I affirm this (your desire) or **something better**."

Only you can create your perfect world, not God nor man. Only you can create your perfect world.

Examples of Positive Affirmations

1. I can do all things through Christ who strengthens me.

2. I commit to the Lord all that I do, and my plans succeed.

3. I delight myself in the Lord; and he gives me the desires of my heart.

4. I seek first the kingdom of God and His righteousness, and all these other things are added to me.

5. I have been raised with Christ, and I seek those things that are above.

6. I am being conformed daily into the image of Christ.

7. I accomplish all that the Father has given me to do.

8. I am a reflection of Christ.

9. I walk by faith and not by sight.

10. I overcome the world by faith.

11. I please God because I live by faith.

12. I am more than a conqueror through Christ who loves me.

13. I am the light of the world and I do not walk in darkness.

14. My God supplies all of my needs.

15. My God has given me the power to create wealth.

16. My effectual and fervent prayers avail much.

17. I am prosperous and pleasing to the Lord.

18. The fullness of the earth belongs to me because I am in Christ Jesus.

19. Whatever I ask the Father in Jesus' name, He gives me.

20. I ask and I receive, that my joy may be full.

21. I love Jesus and God loves me.

22. I receive the wealth of the wicked.

23. My heritage and wealth of the wicked is a gift from God.

24. I prosper and am in great health, just as my soul prospers.

25. God supplies all of my needs according to His riches in Glory by Christ Jesus.

26. I seek the Lord and I do not want for any good thing.

27. The Lord is my shepherd and I shall not want.

28. My generous soul is made rich.

29. I am the temple of the living God.

30. I walk in the spirit and I do not fulfill the desires of the flesh.

Remember when affirming:

Affirm in the positive

First person (I); make it personal

Feelings (get energized)

Idea must be specific

Remain brief

Must be in the present tense

Something better

RECAP
RELEASE

Jesus successfully overcame the
Destructive Erroneous Views In Limitation
by the power of His Word.

- Defined Release and the 5 types of Release

- Identified the 3 major strongholds everyone encounters in life

- Discussed how to overcome the strongholds of life using positive affirmations

Notes

EXPANSION

Discuss the Expansion Process

- Uncover our belief system

- Define the different flows of being

- Discuss the Have & Have Not principle

- Define the 3 stages of "asking"

- Describe the world's paradigm of success

- Describe the Creator's paradigm of success

We are now ready to step into the expansion process. Before we do, it's important that we honestly and prayerfully uncover our belief systems.

I want to share a story with you that demonstrates the importance of an accurate belief system. There once was a farmer whose horse ran away. His neighbor came to comfort him, but the old man replied, "Who knows what is good and what is bad?"

A few days later, the spirited stallion joined a herd of wild mares, leading them back to the farm. The neighbor called on the farmer to share in his joy, but the farmer said, "Who knows what is good and what is bad?"

The following day, while trying to break in one of the wild mares, the farmer's son was thrown and broke his leg. The neighbor joined the farmer to share in his sorrow, but the old man's attitude remained steadfast.

The following week, the army passed by, forcibly recruiting soldiers for a war, but they did not take the farmer's son because he could not walk. The neighbor called on the farmer to congratulate him, but the old, wise farmer said, "Who knows what is good and what is bad?" ~Buddhist Proverb

Let's get back to uncovering our belief systems. The first technique involves taking an honest look at our current belief systems. You do this by looking at your life and seeing what beliefs may have contributed to it. As a way to demonstrate, if there are things that you like and do not like in your life, list them now. Get a piece of paper and write them down. You may have a list that reads something like this: "I have a wonderful family life. I enjoy running and I am good runner. I am a good person. I am a good friend."

"Things I don't like: I am not financially secure. I hate my job! I never get what I want! I am overweight and I feel unhealthy."

Now, look at your lists and ask yourself, "What would a person who created these things have to believe in order to create this life?" This question is especially important in the areas of the things that you don't like. What would I have to believe in order to not be financially secure, to hate my job, to never get what I want, to be overweight and feel unhealthy. What beliefs contribute to that type of lifestyle? Then we begin to understand that life is nothing more than a manifestation of one's beliefs.

So it is very important to spend a few minutes taking an honest look at your life and writing out the good as well as the bad. After doing so, what we must do is write out the type of life that we desire, taking those things such as being financially insecure, hating one's job, never getting what one wants, and being overweight or unhealthy, and writing out your life the way that you desire it. Here are some examples.

When you write out something that you want, it obviously means that you do not have it now. For example, if you wanted to earn a million dollars, it's evident that you do not have a million dollars at this moment. So, what would keep you from earning a million dollars? Because if you truly believed that you could have it, then you would have it.

What are some of your beliefs about money? Do you believe that money is the root of all evil? Do you believe that only rich people have money and that rich people are evil? Do you believe that money is not spiritual?

You see, your beliefs about money determine the amount of money that you have in your life. Once you recognize those beliefs that are keeping you from experiencing the life to which you were destined, you can remove those beliefs and exchange them with positive beliefs. Moreover, that is what the expansion process is all about. By turning your negative beliefs into positive beliefs and affirming those beliefs daily, you will begin to see your world transformed. Here is an example of taking a negative belief and turning it into a positive belief. "I never get what I want." Re-write that belief to say, "I always get what I want."

As we move further along, we will discuss the Expansion Process and we will define the different flows of being; we will discuss the "have and have-not" principle.

We will define the three stages of "asking." We will describe the world's paradigm of success, and we will describe the Creator's paradigm of success.

The Flows of Being

We operate out of one of two paradigms. The first is "<u>Have Do Be</u>," and the other "<u>Be Do Have</u>." The latter is the paradigm of success.

Once you realize that it isn't in the "having" but in the "being" or "becoming" that you are made complete, a whole new world will open up to you. Example: You are a great employee. Great employees do great work and therefore you are able to achieve outstanding results in all of your duties. Your performance is a by-product of who you are, but you are perfect no matter what your performance may be. God says that He knew you even in your mother's womb. He formed you and He pre-ordained you for greatness. So greatness is not based on outward appearance or results. Now, outward appearance and results are based on the greatness you have within you once you unlock and unleash the power of the Christ mind within you. An ancient text says that men look on the outward appearance, but God looks at the heart.

Incorrect Flow of Being
Fear-based beliefs with feelings

HAVE (Physical)	DO (Transition)	BE (Spiritual)
EFFECT	ACTION	CAUSE
LACK	WITHHOLD	FEARFUL

As stated earlier, we operate within one of two paradigms: a paradigm of fear or a paradigm of faith. The first paradigm is an incorrect flow of being. We call this the "have-do-be" mentality. "Having" is always the physical manifestation of "doing," which is a byproduct of "being." "Be" or "being" is a spiritual manifestation of what we are–the true essence of who we are. We call this the "cause."

Say, for example, you are operating out of a mindset of lack, loss, and limitation. That mindset says, "I never get what I want. I am in debt and more debt is coming." What must one believe in order to manifest these results? You believe in what it is that you have. So because you believe in lack, loss and limitation, your "doing" is withholding. The Word says, "Do not withhold good when it is in your power to do it." Because you operate out of a "lack" mentality, you withhold good, whether it is praise, money, or whatever you're capable of giving.

Now, the reason why you are withholding that good, why you're manifesting that action, is because your state of being or becoming is that of fear or fearfulness. As you operate out of the incorrect flow based on "having," not "being," you manifest lack, loss and limitation. But when we change the flow of being, we see a radical transformation in the life that we are living.

Correct Flow of Being
Faith-based beliefs with feelings

BE (Spiritual)	DO (Transition)	HAVE (Physical)
CAUSE	ACTION	EFFECT
FAITH	GIVE	INCREASE

The be-do-have sequence is much more successful since it involves growth from within. The first step is to become, in your state of being, the thing you desire. This means to consciously associate with the thing you desire. Along the way, you will draw to you the things you desire.

When we operate out of the correct flow of being, we operate out of faith (the spiritual realm). We operate out of a "be-do-have," with "be," again, being spiritual. We operate out of our true self. And we begin "doing," or "transitioning," the action of that based on what we know in the knowledge of our true self. Then we begin to attract the things that we desire. Because we understand coming from the "being" that everything we desire, we become in our very nature, in our very core, in our very self. Millionaires! Writers! Speakers! We attract to ourselves better jobs because we understand that we are that energy that we are sending out. We send out our intentions or expectations so the cause is one of faith in the creation process of the universe. We realize that "we can do all things through Christ who strengthens us."

What are the effects? What do we have? We have now that million dollars. We have now that job that we have always desired. We have now that more abundant life. We now have increase, because we are operating out of the correct flow of being.

It's like the Christian experience. Many of us struggle for years to be Christians. We say, "If I could just do this right! If I could just pray hard enough. If I could just _____ " (*you fill in the blank*). But once we understand our identity as children and brothers and sisters in the Body of Christ, we begin to operate out of the love of God, not the fear of God. We begin to understand that because Christ gave Himself for us, we have been grafted into the family of God. We are no longer called servants, but "friend." He calls us brothers and sisters in the Body of Christ.

And we become those who can ask our desires of the Father. The Word says it is done unto us, and that is so, because we now understand the mind of God and because we are in the Word of God, meditating and contemplating and letting that Word dwell in us richly. But we understand–because of relationships, not religion–that we are operating out of a state of being. And because we are Christ's workmanship in the earth, and because we are Christ's ambassadors in the earth, we know we can ask anything of the Father, even as Christ asked of the Father, and it was done according to His Word.

Have and Have Not

*H*ave not, ask not (James 4:2)

*A*sk amiss (James 4:3)

*V*oid of having results (Mark 4:25b)

*E*xperience the results of having (Mark 4:25a)

When we are operating out of a state of be-ing, we know that we can ask the Father whatever it is that we desire and it will be manifested in our lives. This is because we do not ask solely for ourselves, but we are seeking to manifest His Glory in the world. And in that, we begin to awaken to the per-son that God has called us to be.

So you ask the question, "Why is it that I do not have, in my life, the things that I've asked for?" And we are going to talk about the principles of having and having not. If we go to James 4:2-3, James first says that you "have not" because you ask not. Many of us simply fail to have because we fail to ask. It is as simple as that. We fail to understand that God wishes to give us the desires of our heart.

Secondly, many of us fail to have because we ask "amiss." Now you may say, "Well, I did, in fact, ask." Perhaps, but you asked with the wrong motives. You asked solely for yourself. God does not mind blessing you. You cannot be a conduit of water and not get wet. So, as God begins to bless others through you, the by-product is that you will also be blessed.

King Solomon asked for wisdom that he might serve God's people. And God said to Solomon, "Since you asked for wisdom to shepherd my people, I will bless you not only with wisdom but with wellness and wealth." Solomon understood this principle because of the teachings of his father. If you read the Psalms, David continuously says, "In all your getting, get understanding." Throughout the Proverbs, we read Solomon challenging us to do likewise.

David, Solomon's father, had already planted the seed: "Solomon, get wisdom!" So when God asked Solomon, "What is it that you desire of me?" Solomon said, "Give me wisdom that I may shepherd your people." And God blessed him three-fold, with wisdom, wellness and wealth.

Again, seek to be a conduit of blessing. You can't be a conduit of blessing and not be blessed any more than you can be conduit of water and not get wet.

We have talked about "ask not, have not." We have also mentioned asking amiss. Now we're ready to discuss the void of having results. You might say, "What does that mean?" In Mark 4:25, Jesus talks about two people. He says for he who has, more will be given. And from he who has not, even that which he has will be taken away. The question, referring to the one who is void of having results, indicates that even that which he has will be taken away if he does not have. The truth of the matter is, many of us operate out of a double-mindedness in the Body of Christ. We say, "I want to be wealthy," but then we say, "Well, rich people are stingy. Rich people are tyrants. You can't trust them–they're thieves, they're liars!" And we have a mixed message going on in our mind.

We talked about it earlier, and I'll touch on it briefly again. We have within us something called a reticular activating system. This is just a complex way of saying that we have something in us that won't allow us to think two opposing thoughts at the same time. You can't think about having a million dollars and hate rich people. You can't talk about being healthy, and despise someone that is health-conscious. You must begin to align your mind with the things that you desire in your life.

Henry Ford said it this way, "Whether you think you can, or you think you can't--you're right." So whatever it is that you think about, you bring about. Earl Nightingale said that you become what you think about most of the time. The Bible says it this way: "as a man thinks in his heart, so is he." Whatever your predominant thought is and what you think about with feeling, whether it be that of faith or fear, you bring about. Many of you are void of having   results primarily because of the way you think. If you begin to change your thinking about what you believe is possible in your life; if you begin to praise those who are prospering; if you take on an attitude of gratitude, you will find yourself becoming a conduit of wisdom, wellness and wealth. You will see your divine nature attributes attracting to you all the things that you desire.

In Mark 4:24, Jesus said, "Take heed of what you hear, and the measure that you give will be given back to you. And even more will be given to you." This is speaking of the person who is experiencing "having." Having always begins in the mental realm and is manifested in the physical realm. Ultimately, this is where all creation begins. Know with certainly that everything God has for you is being manifested, and that you are a conduit of God's blessing, not only for your life but for the lives of others. You want to be a healer; you want to be able to heal people with your words; you want to be able to speak life into the lives of others; you want to be able to give away prosperity into the lives of others, because what it is that you send out bounces back on the universal mirror and reflects back to you. But it doesn't reflect back to you solely what you sent out. It bounces back to you, or reflects back to you, whatever it is you are sending out multiplied. And it goes back to when Jesus said that he who has given up family, loved ones, a house, etc. in this life will receive a hundred times more in this life and eternal life in the life to come.

This is how the universe is designed. You can't sow a seed of prosperity and reap a seed. You reap a hundred-fold, a thousand-fold, and ten-thousand fold. Whatever it is that you are sending out, it is returning to you. So, creator, what is it that you are creating this very moment? Become a conscious creator. This is the goal of the creation process—that you become a conscious creator; that you become Christ in the earth. We are to be Christ's extension. He says go out and make disciples of all nations. And we are called Christians, Christ-like, or Christ. Let us not miss our calling to be life transformers in this twenty-first century.

3 Stages of Asking

*A*sk Boldly (Heb 4:16 & James 1:5)

*S*eek Emotional Alignment (James 1:8 & Phil 2:5)

*K*now You Have Your Answers (Mark 11:24)

We will now discuss the three stages of "asking." The first stage of asking is to **ask boldly**. From the Word of God, in the book of James 1, verse 5: "If any of you lack wisdom, let him ask God who gives all men generously without reproaching and it will be given him." And in the book of Hebrews, Heb. 4:16, it says that we must ask boldly! We must come to the throne room of Grace and ask boldly in our time of need.

So first of all, we must ask, petition God, and we must do it with a sense of boldness, realizing that when He sees us, He doesn't see "YOU." He sees His Son,

Jesus. He sees the Christ in you, and He says, "Whatever you desire, my child, it is given to you. Not because of you, but because of Christ who dwells within you."

Next we must *seek emotional alignment* with God's Word. And what does that mean, emotional alignment? In James 1:8, it says that the double-minded person must not suppose that he will receive anything from God. The double-minded person is unstable in all of his ways. So we can't be those people who are swinging between two opinions. We must believe the Word of God upon our lives, and we must begin to walk in that, with that sense of boldness, realizing that we can ask anything of the Father and that it will be done according to our beliefs.

In Philippians 2:5, we are told to have this mind in us, which was also in Jesus. And I can't emphasize enough–that's what the creation process is all about: understanding that you now have the mind of Christ. And because you have the mind of Christ, you are now God's ambassadors in the earth. And you can do the very thing that Christ did and more. He said, "Even greater works will you do, if you believe." Do you believe that you are Christ's representation in the earth? If so, begin to live as such.

And this takes us into the last stage of asking. **Know** that your prayers are answered. It's much like when Lazarus died and Jesus went to the tomb and He said, "Father, I'm not asking you because I need to see the manifestation. But I'm asking you to make this right by raising Lazarus from the dead, for those who are watching, that they may glorify your name." We ask, knowing that our prayers are answered for the Glory of God.

Let's go to Mark 11:24. Jesus says, "Therefore, I tell you whatever you ask in prayer, believe that you have received it." Received what? Whatever you asked in prayer will be yours. As stated earlier, many of us are devoid of the results of "having" because of double-mindedness. It was stated early in the Bible that many of the children of Israel did not enter into the Promised Land because of unbelief. Many of us are not entering into the promises of God for this generation because of unbelief.

But Jesus said whatever you ask in prayer, believing, will be yours.

My question to you, creator, is, "What are you asking for or failing to ask for?" Once you understand that the manifestation in your life is not God's doing, but your own doing, and when you begin to step out in faith, and begin to walk out the power of the Christ-life in your life, you will begin to manifest a life once only imagined in your dreams. It is available to you now, creator! Ask boldly, seek emotional alignment, and know that your prayers are answered.

I want to share a poem with you on the power of asking.

When I Ask

When I ask I do not wish, I KNOW. I do not dream, I STATE. I do not hope, I AC-CEPT. I do not pray, I PROCLAIM. I do not expect something is going to happen, I BELIEVE THAT IT HAS ALREADY HAPPENED. ~Anonymous

Creator's Eyes

The primary goal of this book is to awaken the creator within you. Remember that the world operates out of a "have-do-be" mentality and this is a paradigm of fear. The paradigm of success is be-do-have; this is when you are operating out of a paradigm of faith and when you're most like your Creator.

Everything that is manifested in the world is first created in the mind. Manifestation never begins in the physical realm. This would be a backwards flow of being. Your desired outcome begins with your thought, creator! You have created your life and the world that you see. You have created your present reality. You need only to change the way you're thinking if you desire to create something different. The moment you begin to think differently is the very moment your life will begin to change. But, creator, you must begin to think differently!

Life changes from the perspective of a creator. Expansion is nothing more than seeing life from a Christ perspective, a divine perspective, and a God perspective. We recognize that all reality begins in the mind and is then manifested. With creative exchange, we are able to impact our environment and our world, and our very circumstances cause events to happen and attract money and possessions into our lives. We attract to us the type of work and love that we desire for ourselves. We change habits and even improve our state of health. It is the power behind every success story.

Where is the power? The power is within us all! The power is in you! You are the creator of the world that you are presently experiencing. I'm not talking about the things going on outside of you. I'm talking about how you are perceiving life at this very moment. Through past thinking, you have created the things that you have attracted into your life. You are responsible for that! And as you begin to think differently, you'll begin to manifest different results in your life. But you are responsible, creator! Only you can create your perfect world, not God nor man only you can create your perfect world!

RECAP
EXPANSION

- Uncovered our belief system

- Defined the different flows of being

- Discussed the Have & Have Not principle

- Defined the 3 stages of "asking"

- Described the world's paradigm of success

- Described the Creator's paradigm of success

Notes

ALLOWING

Begin to Utilize the Power of Allowing

- Define Allowing

- Discuss benefits in Allowing

- Execute an Allowing exercise

- Define the 4 types of Allowers

DEFINE ALLOWING

"Allowing" is nothing more than forming a clear mental picture of the things that you desire most in life. Vague wants produce vague results. The more specific you get, the more specific your results. Remember that God has created the universe like a giant copy machine. Whatever you send out to the universe in continual thought form will return to you in physical manifestation. If you're sending out lack, loss and limitation, then lack, loss and limitation is what's being sent back to you.

The words that we speak and the thoughts that we think produce life or death, faith or fear. We talked earlier about the keys of the kingdom, but it is important that we repeat it again here. Jesus said, "I will give you the keys of the kingdom of heaven. Whatever you bind on earth will be bound in heaven, and whatever you loose on earth will be loosed in heaven."

Jesus affirms the concept of the giant copy machine of the universe. See, whatever it is that we send out, whatever things that we say that we can and cannot do, the universe agrees with us. So we must be mindful of what we allow in the universe. Because whatever it is that we are sending out, we will surely manifest. Understand that you have been created in the image of God. And that means that first and foremost, you are a creator.

Benefits of Allowing

What does relaxation, good health, financial prosperity or peace of mind look like to you? You can have what you think through the Allowing process.

What are the benefits of being an "allower" or creator? The words that we speak either produce life or death, faith or fear. Since we will give an account for every idle word, according to Christ, we should be more mindful of the words that we use, not only with our neighbors but with ourselves. Notice what the Bible says: life and death are in the power of the tongue. And they that love it shall eat the fruit thereof.

Creator, my question to you is, "What fruits are you manifesting in your life today?" Understand that life and death are in the power of your tongue. And before they hit your tongue, they must first and foremost hit your thoughts. So we must be mindful of the things that we think about as creators and understand that everything we think about has an end. And it will yield a harvest! It will produce! So, as you begin to meditate and control your thoughts, you will begin to understand that there is no such thing as an "idle thought."   What gives rise to whole worlds, universes and galaxies can hardly be called "idle!" You are a creator!

EXERCISE

Here we are going into the process of executing an allowing exercise. I suggest that you do this at least once a day for 5-10 minutes. First, you must form a clear mental picture of the things you desire to do and/or become. You must hold this mental picture in your mind with a spirit of expectancy. Divine intelligence does not compete—it creates. It functions effortlessly

with harmony and love. And when you har-
ness the force of harmony and love, you
create success and good fortune with effort-
less ease.

Another way to allow is to write down a
list of your desires in their order of importance. Remember, you cannot desire too
much! We serve a God who gives more
than we can ask, think and/or imagine. So
when you write your list, go for it! Do not
be discouraged on the account of change.
You desire change from time to time, so re-
adjust and move forward.

Once you have your list, there are three
things that you should do. First, you must
read from your list of desires three times a
day, preferably morning, noon and night.
Second, you must think of what you desire
as often as possible. It must become a part
of you at the cellular level. It must be so
much a part of you that it's not even a desire any longer; it's a part of who you are,
and you are just waiting on the manifestation because you know that it's coming.
Third, do not talk to anyone about your desire, except for your heavenly Father. And
He says, speak to Him in the secret place,
in the closet, and He will reward you
openly.

At first, this will seem like wishful thinking. But as you move forward, you will begin to see the manifestation of your desire. Now, I'm sure that many of you question how long you shall perform this process. You do it until you manifest your desire or until your desire changes.

4 Types of Allowers

Powerless Allower – chaotic creator (Matt 13:19)

"The seeds that fell along the road are the people who hear the message of truth, but not understand it. Then through ignorance, allow the message to be snatched from their hearts."

Premature Allower – coincidental creator (Matt 13:20-21)

"The seeds that fell on rocky ground are the people who gladly hear the message and accept it right away. But they don't have deep roots, and they don't last very long. As soon as life gets hard or they get in trouble, they give up."

Practical Allower – cautious creator
(Matt 13:22)

"The seeds that fell among the thorn bushes are also people who hear the message. But they start worrying about the needs of this life and are fooled by self-indulgent interests. So the message gets choked out, and they never produce anything."

Purposeful Allower – conscious creator
(Matt 13:23)

"The seeds that fell on good ground are the people who hear and understand the message. They produce as much as thirty, sixty and a hundred times what was planted."

Powerless Allower

The powerless allower or chaotic creator has no time, he says, to think on spiritual matters. The road of his heart is a congested superhighway. He has no desires concerning spiritual matters, nor is he affected by anything spiritual in nature. He, like the superhighway, was never intended to be a garden. If a single grain of truth should fall on his heart and grow and rest for a while upon his thoughts, he would forget all that he has heard when a more agreeable form of distraction has captured his attention.

The powerless allower has no idea that he is an allower. He believes that life is just a matter of happenchance or fate. He believes that doing his best is the key to his success. He believes his thoughts play little or no part in his success. He believes if there is a God, He isn't interested in him. He always seems to get the raw end of the deal. His motto is, "Get them before they get me!"

Premature Allower

The premature allower or coincidental creator has a more pliable heart concerning spiritual matters. He tends to be more impressible. While other men see nothing in the teaching of truth, this man weeps. He has hopes, but his vacillation keeps him from consistently bringing about his desired end. Often a seeker of truth, when the message of truth penetrates his heart, he rejoices. But his elation is short-lived. As another passage explains it: "And these are they likewise which are sown on stony ground; who, when they have heard the word, immediately receive it with gladness; and have no root in themselves, and so endure but for a time: afterward, when affliction or persecution arises for the word's sake, immediately they are offended."

The premature allower is more likely to be a seeker of truth. He may find himself attracted to so-called spiritual teaching. He is easily moved by the things of the spirit. If his teacher teaches earnestly, he feels it, and loves him, and rallies behind him, much to his teacher's delight. But time, which proves all things, proves him. This allower's joy is an untimely birth. He seems to be made of true substance; but when he is put to the test of fire, he is consumed in the furnace of indecision.

Practical Allower

The practical allower or cautious creator hears the word of truth and understands what he hears. He takes the truth home; he thinks it over; he even goes as far as to become a religious practitioner. But he never matures in the perfection of the truth, having a form of godliness but denying its power. This individual has a great deal to see after; he has the cares of the world on his shoulders. Be not deceived by his apparent godliness—he has no time for it. He will tell you he lives in the real world; that he cannot neglect his duties; that he must look to the business at hand, and his family's future and eternity will take care of itself. He is too earthly-minded to be any heavenly good.

The practical allower is often successful by the world's standard of success. He drives the finest car and lives in the most expensive home in the best neighborhood. He doesn't have a care in the world. He has everything his heart can imagine. He doesn't say, "Where will the money come from to pay these bills?" or "How shall I provide for my growing family?" He has more material goods than the heart could desire. He has become so wealthy that he has forgotten how to be gracious.

You may believe that God does not have a plan for your life. But when you begin to seek God's purpose for your life, you will move beyond the powerless, premature, practical allowers to become a purposeful allower.

Purposeful Allower

One out of four people who receive the word of truth is a purposeful allower. Down fell the seed to take good root. In some cases, it produced fervency of love, peace and joy. These seeds produce some thirty, sixty and a hundredfold. This individual is a mighty servant of truth. He accomplishes deeds of daring which few accomplish. *"The people who know their God shall be strong and do great exploits"* (Dan 11:32). The seed has fallen in the good ground. Soul, thy petition will be heard. God never gives a man a desire without intending to bring about its manifestation.

My prayer for you, who doesn't believe that God has a purpose for your life, is that you will begin seeking God's plan for your life by faith. I'll ask you what God asked Moses, "What's in your hand?" Begin there.

Purposeful allower knows in his heart of hearts that God has a purpose for him, and he begins to live out life with God's purpose in mind; even though he may not have the complete picture, he operates and walks in what he knows.

Once you begin to understand what your gifts are, what your talents are, what your bent is in or towards, you'll begin to move out and become a purposeful allower using your gifts and your talents for the Glory of God. And as you obey moment by moment in the now, God will begin to reveal to you more and more of what His purpose and plan is for your life; and you'll begin to allow a life of purpose.

RECAP
ALLOWING

- Defined Allowing

- Discussed benefits in Allowing

- Executed an Allowing exercise

- Described the 4 types of Allowers

Notes

TRANSFORMATION

Discuss the Transformation Process

- Define Transformation

- Discuss the four stages of Transformation

- Discuss steps in the Transformation process

- Define the ten Transformational affirmations

DEFINE TRANSFORMATION

Change your mind and change your world. Inherent in every intention and desire is the mechanism for its fulfillment. Intention plus desire, when acted upon, will bring about an infinite potentiality to its possessor. It is only as you act upon intention and desire that transformation can and will take place. Intention and desire are nothing more than wishful thinking without the introduction of action.

4 Levels of Transformation

1. Unconscious incompetence

2. Conscious incompetence

3. Conscious competence

4. Unconscious competence

"And be not conformed to this world: but be transformed by the renewing of your mind" (Romans 12:2).

There are four basic steps your mind sub-consciously follows in the process of trans-formational learning.

Unconscious Incompetence

The first step is Unconscious Incompe-tence. At the very beginning, you are in a state of unconscious incompetence. You are completely ignorant of the laws and principles in question, and you do not know what you do not know. We will use the ex-ample of tying one's shoe. A baby does not know that it does not know how to ties its shoe until it gets to a certain age.

Conscious Incompetence

Then there is Conscious Incompetence. This is when you learn or you hear of the laws, but you haven't yet attempted to ap-ply them. You are in a state of conscious incompetence. You are aware that you do not understand, and you may or may not choose to do anything about it.

Conscious Competence

The next stage is Conscious Competence. This is when you deliberately decide to apply the universal laws and techniques learned in this book. But you have to consciously think through every step. This is a state of conscious competence. You know that you know but you still have to consciously apply that wisdom. It is like you have just learned how to drive a manual car. You can certainly do it, but you still have to think about the decision in acting and driving that car.

Unconscious Competence

Then you reach a state of "expertise," or what we call Unconscious Competence. Ultimately, when you reach the stage of unconscious competence, you are on automatic pilot. The techniques and principles have become so ingrained that they are habitual. You do not even have to consciously think about them. You are on auto-pilot. It is much like breathing. It is so ingrained in your subconscious mind that you're at a state of alternate personal power, and we call this "creation."

Transformation Table

Unconscious	Incompetence	Don't know you don't know	**W**ithout a clue
Conscious	Incompetence	Know you don't know	**A**wareness
Conscious	Competence	Know you know	**K**nowledge
Unconscious	Competence	Do without conscious thought	**E**xpertise

TEN TRANSFORMATIONAL AFFIRMATIONS

1. I acknowledge apart from my Father (God) I can do nothing. (John 5:19)

2. I observe what my Father (God) is doing and I do likewise. (John 5:19)

3. My Father (God) and I are one. (John 10:30)

4. I can do all things through God (Christ) who strengthens me. (Phil 4:13)

5. I cast down every imagination that exalts itself against the knowledge of Christ. (2 Cor. 10:5)

6. I am only forgiven to the extent in which I'm willing to forgive. (Mat 18:35)

7. Every day in every way I'm becoming better and better. (2 Cor. 3:18)

8. I am being conformed into the image of Christ daily. (Rom 8:29)

9. I have been created for greatness. (Jer. 1:5)

10. I am a reflection of Christ in the world. (1 John 4:13)

RECAP
TRANSFORMATION

- Defined Transformation

- Discussed the four stages of Transformation

- Discussed steps in the Transformation process

- Defined the ten affirmations of Transformation

Notes

OPULENCE

Discuss the Opulence Process

- Define Opulence

- Identify the five stages of Opulence

  1. Opulence through positioning

  2. Opulence through prioritization

  3. Opulence through petitioning

  4. Discuss the three ways the Creator answers prayer

  5. Unleashing blessings through praise and gratitude

DEFINE OPULENCE

What you sow is what you reap. When we choose actions that bring happiness and success to others, we release happiness and success in our own lives. "You shall have what you say" (Mark 11:23-24).

Identify the Five Stages of Opulence

Positioning

The first stage of obtaining opulence is positioning. First, we must be in a position to receive the blessing of our heavenly Father. And in order to do this, we must be in the family of God, joint heirs with Christ. Think about it! That's quite a position to be in. We must share in the inheritance of Christ. "All is yours and all is Christ's and all is God's" (I Cor. 3:23).

Prioritization

The second stage is prioritization. We must be sure that our priorities are in order so that our requests will be in keeping with God's will. "But seek ye first the kingdom of God and His righteousness, and all these things will be added unto you" (Matthew 6:33).

Petition

The third stage is asking. We must spend time with the Lord in prayer so that we can share our desires with Him and let Him know our requests. And asking: "Ask, and it shall be given unto you. Seek and you shall find. Knock and the door shall be opened" (Matthew 7:7).

Perception

The fourth stage is perception. "Do not judge according to appearance, but judge righteously" (John 7:24).

Life is not always as it appears, as Jesus experienced in the Garden of Gethsemane.

He said, "If it be possible, let this cup pass from Me, but not My will; but Your will be done" (Matt. 26:39).

God's "Y.E.S." comes in one of three ways. First, God will answer with an immediate answer, "YES." Second, God will answer with, "Not now, but 'EVENTUALLY.'" Third, God will not answer with a "no" but "SOMETHING BETTER," as stated in the Garden of Gethsemane. Because we are God's children, He has something far better in store for us as well.

Think of your most extravagant thoughts and then try to think of something far beyond them. Even if you have a crystal-clear imagination, there will still be a limit to what you are able to envision.

However, your Father does not have the same limitations that you have. He says that He is able to do immeasurably MORE than anything that you could ask, think or imagine. The sky is the limit as far as He is concerned. He knows no earthly barriers or boundaries that will keep Him from fulfilling the best plans and purposes for you, His child.

Praise

In the fifth stage, thank God for His answer and for His blessing. "We are to give thanks always for all things unto God and the Father in the name of our Lord Jesus Christ" (Eph 5:20).

The fifth stage is releasing the blessings of God through an attitude of gratitude, giving thanks for all things to God the Father, in the name of our Lord Jesus Christ. There is nothing as powerful as an attitude of gratitude to unleash the power of God in one's life. He stated it this way: "Prove Me, Lord of Hosts, and see if I will not open the windows of heaven and pour out a blessing that there shall not be room enough to receive it" (Malachi 3:10).

Only you can create your perfect world; not God nor man, only you can create your perfect world.

RECAP
OPULENCE

- Defined Opulence

- Identified the five stages of Opulence

    1. Discussed Opulence through positioning

    2. Discussed Opulence through prioritization

    3. Discussed Opulence through petitioning

    4. Discussed the three ways the Creator answers prayer

    5. Discussed unleashing blessings through praise and gratitude

Notes

RE-CREATION
Discuss the Re-creation Process

- Define Re-creation

- Identify the five stages of successful Re-creation

  1. Re-creation through modeling

  2. Re-creation through mentoring

  3. Re-creation through monitoring

  4. Re-creation through motivation

  5. Re-creation through multiplication

DEFINE RE-CREATION

Re-creation is nothing more than sharing the principles and truths you have learned in this book with others. It is preferred that you share with those who are seeking to create their desired world as a result of applying the principles herein. Like you, they will begin to notice their whole world being transformed into the world they have imagined.

Now that you understand the process, how do you go about teaching others in this life-changing process? In his book "Developing the Leaders around You," John Maxwell describes a five-step process to equip potential leaders. We will utilize this process to transform the creators around us.

Modeling

You first re-create through modeling, by living out the Creation process while the pupil watches you. It is important that he sees the whole process from start to finish, or what we call the "cradle to the grave."

Mentoring

The next stage is the mentoring phase. Here you can live out the re-creation process, but the pupil you are training comes alongside you, following your example. You must explain to the pupil not only the "hows" but the "whys" of each step.

Monitoring

The next stage is monitoring. Now it is time to trade places. The student performs a task while you observe whether or not it is correct. It is important that you empower and encourage through this process. Continue to work with him until he has consistency and ask him to explain the process to you, for it will help him to understand it better.

Motivating

The next step is motivating. In this step, you take yourself out of the process and let the student begin to create for himself, making sure he knows how to go through the process with no aid from you. Continue to encourage him and stay with him until he senses success. Now he may wish to improve the process and encourage him to do so—and learn from him.

Multiplying

The final stage is multiplying. Once the new creator is awakened, and says and does an outstanding job with the process, it becomes his turn to teach others to create their perfect worlds. For you, it is an opportunity to see the new creator and give him or her more ability by teaching others to show what he or she has learned. And this is what the "creation" process is all about. Taking one and teaching him so that he may teach others.

RECAP
RE-CREATION

- Defined Re-creation

- Identified the five stages of successful Re-creation

  1. Re-creation through modeling

  2. Re-creation through mentoring

  3. Re-creation through monitoring

  4. Re-creation through motivation

  5. Re-creation through multiplication

Notes

The 7 Steps of Personal Creation

We have covered the seven-step process of personal creation. In this seven-step procedure, we have discovered the tools for successful conscious creation utilizing the acronym "CREATOR."

The letter "**C**" stands for "Consciousness."

The letter "**R**" stands for "Release."

The letter "**E**" stands for "Expansion."

The letter "**A**" stands for "Allowing."

The letter "**T**" stands for "Transformation."

The letter "**O**" stands for "Opulence."

The letter "**R**" stands for "Re-creation."

As you embark on your life's journey remember that you alone are responsible for the change you desire. No one else can make the change for you. Only you can begin the process of change in your life. Dare to think, believe, and dream of a life that only a few dare to imagine. The universe being no respecter of person rewards each one according to his or her thoughts.

The Great Commission

*All authority has been given to you in the spiritual, mental and physical realm. You are to go therefore and make students throughout the world, teaching them the principles of the creation process, teaching them to observe all that you have learned in this book: "**God and the Law of Attraction**."*

"God loved the people of this world so much that He gave His only Son, so that everyone who has faith in Him will live forever" (John 3:16).

About the Author

DeCarlo A. Eskridge is a spiritual life-coach/ trainer, motivational speaker, certified hypno-therapist, certified N.L.P. practitioner, author, and minister. He is very proud to have authored and independently-published several books through his company NU DAE Enterprises where he serves as President and CEO.

A prolific teacher and encourager, DeCarlo A. Eskridge reads over 50 books a year, and listens to countless hours of audio programs. He is a Certified Life Coach through Franklin Covey and a motivational speaker who earned advanced honors at Toastmasters International. He is also an Ordained Minister with over 25 years of biblical study.

DeCarlo A. Eskridge has been imbued with an inexhaustible, unyielding, and unre-lenting thirst and hunger for knowledge. His mission is to travel the globe teaching, em-powering, inspiring, and transforming the lives of millions with the truths he has discovered in order that every person recognizes who he or she is, what he or she can accomplish, and that they live it!

DeCarlo A. Eskridge is married with two stepsons. His lovely wife Amanda, Executive Vice President and Public Relations Manager of NU DAE Enterprises, works collaboratively with him as a counselor, spiritual life-coach/ trainer, motivational speaker, co-author and minister.

NU DAE Enterprise Publications

DeCarloEskridge.com

Amazon — Create Space
ISBN-13: 978-1463644734
ISBN-10: 1463644736